D0406458

An Educator's Guide
to Finding Resources
in the Public Domain

KENYON DAVID POTTER

Phi Delta Kappa Educational Foundation
Bloomington, Indiana U.S.A.

Cover design by
Victoria Voelker

Phi Delta Kappa Educational Foundation
408 North Union Street
Post Office Box 789
Bloomington, Indiana 47402-0789
U.S.A.

Printed in the United States of America

This book is intended solely as a guide for educators and should not be construed as legal advice. The information herein should not be relied on as a substitute for, or in lieu of, consultation with a copyright professional or attorney. The author and the publisher have made significant efforts to ensure the accuracy of the contents at the time of publication. However, no warranty, express or implied, is made.

Library of Congress Catalog Card Number 99-70206
ISBN 0-87367-815-X
Copyright © 1999 by Kenyon David Potter
All rights reserved

To my wife, Irma

Acknowledgments

I would like to thank the staff of the United States Copyright Office in Washington, D.C., and the reference librarians at public libraries in the San Francisco Bay Area, who provided answers to many questions during my research and offered leads to many of the resources listed in this book. I also would like to thank all of those individuals who contribute to the establishment and maintenance of online libraries and archives of works in the public domain.

I would like to give special thanks to my mother, who inspired me to be an educator and a writer.

Table of Contents

Introduction

In this book I present a general method for finding educational resources in the public domain. For the uninitiated, the phrase "in the public domain" refers to the contents of works — texts, photographs, graphics — to which no claim of ownership can be made. Works in the public domain may be used by anyone; and educators, in particular, will find that the public domain is a treasure chest of valuable resources for teaching and learning.

Obtaining permission to reproduce a published work often is time-consuming and can be expensive. Even finding the copyright status of a work can be difficult. Thus the purpose of this book is to help educators find creative works in the public domain that can be used without the necessity of obtaining permission from a publisher or other copyright holder.

Works in the public domain fall primarily into two large categories: works never copyrighted and works whose copyright has expired. Most government publications are in the first category, for example. The second category contains many historical works, such as books published a century or more ago.

In principle, all copyrighted works eventually enter the public domain. Copyright is not intended to last forever. "To promote the progress of science and the useful arts," Section 8 of Article I of the U.S. Constitution empowers Congress to enact laws "securing for limited times to authors and inventors the exclusive right to their respective writings and discoveries." Once those "limited times" have expired, such works become public property.

Copyright laws have been changed from time to time and even today remain in flux. Thus it seems reasonable to begin this guide

1

with a summary of current copyright law with respect to public domain issues. With that foundation in place, the subsequent section sets out an 8-step procedure for locating resources and investigating their copyright status. The goal of this procedure is to provide educators with a method for tapping resources clearly in the public domain to use in educational settings.

Finally, in the concluding sections of this guide, I offer suggestions and resources that educators may find useful in prying open the treasure chest of the public domain.

Copyright Protection and the Public Domain

A word of caution is necessary at the outset. No book can possibly remain up-to-date with the rapidity of change in copyright law. I stated in the Introduction that copyright law is in flux. These days, it seems, some piece of legislation related to copyright always is pending. Therefore, the reader must be advised that the information contained herein is general and can be considered only broadly current, subject to recent changes resulting from new legislation.

Definitions

The literal definition of *copyright* is the "right to copy." Copyright is intended to protect a creator's interest in his or her creative works. Such works may be literary, artistic, or intellectual in nature and may pertain to any subject. A work is protected by copyright from the moment it is recorded or "fixed in a tangible form." Thus the act of creation also creates immediate copyright protection.

The term "creative works" covers a vast range of expression, including (but not limited to) written texts, pictorial drawings, photographic images, phonographic recordings, cinemagraphic films, and digital recordings. "Written texts" covers books, essays, articles, plays, and so on, including their expression in nonwritten forms, such as audiovisual matter (videotapes, audiotapes) and live performances. The newest media, such as digital content on

3

computer disks and online, also are covered by copyright. Indeed, one reason that copyright law is in flux is the constant state of change evident in communications technology. As new media emerge, new laws must address how copyright protections can be extended.

Authorship

Most of the time a work's creator can be termed the "author," which is the shorthand reference I will use throughout this guide to include writers, photographers, artists, and other creators of works under copyright. Several points about authorship have a bearing on copyright.

First of all, identity is an issue. Many writers use pseudonyms. For example, Jane Austen published her first novel, *Sense and Sensibility*, simply under the phrase "By a Lady." In her early works, Louisa May Alcott used the pseudonym A. Barnard, and Samuel Langhorne Clemens wrote as Mark Twain. In these famous cases, discerning the author's true identity is a minor problem; but it can complicate checking on copyright if the author is less well-known.

A second issue concerns whether the author is living or dead. Some copyright standards are tied to the year of an author's death, as I will explain shortly.

A third issue is actual copyright ownership. "Copyright by John Doe" on the reverse of a book's title page does not ensure that the copyright is held by John Doe. Many authors' copyright interests are conveyed by contract to another party, often the publisher of the work, who becomes the actual copyright owner. Permission to reproduce all or any portion of a copyrighted work therefore must come from the owner, not necessarily the author.

Alternatively, the author of a work may be an employee whose job is to create works for an employer. Such works are classified as "works for hire," and the employer, not the author, is the copyright owner. In fact, such works may not even identify the actual creator. Government publications are examples of works issued

4

by an organization, such as the Department of Education, for which the author is seldom credited.

Ownership

The owner of a copyright has the absolute "right to copy" the work. This right is the subject of law, and the right may be complete, exclusive, or limited in various ways. Most works are published with "all rights reserved," meaning that the copyright owner can decide who may copy all or a portion of the owned work. For example, the right to copy may be granted conditionally: "for educational purposes," "for not-for-profit purposes," or "for noncommercial purposes."

Rights also involve *copying* in its broadest sense: mechanical copying, photocopying, electronic scanning, recording, broadcasting, and so on — including the storage of works in retrieval systems even when permission has been granted to copy them. A copyright owner may limit copying, for example, to recordings for the blind.

Ownership rights are limited by the doctrine of fair use. Like many provisions in copyright law, fair use is much debated and seems to be constantly reinterpreted. I will touch on fair use matters in a moment; however, educators should not rely on fair use.

For most published works, a starting point for determining copyright ownership is the reverse of a book's title page. The copyright notice usually is printed there, along with the name and address of the work's publisher. The actual notice consists of the word *copyright* — usually followed by the universal copyright symbol © — the year of first publication, and the name of the original copyright holder. Again, the copyright holder may not currently own the copyright, which may have been transferred by contract to someone else. When a publisher "owns" an author's copyright by contract, copyright ownership often reverts to the named holder either when the book is taken out of print or after a specified period of time.

The copyright date refers to the year of publication, which in fact may be years after a work is created. Copyright resides in the work when it is created, whether published or not. Publication is not a requirement of copyright. But for purposes of this guide, my focus will be on published works, because those will more likely be sought as resources by educators. The actual month and day of publication are largely irrelevant.

Duration of Copyright

The duration of copyright protection has changed at various times. Historically, the term of copyright protection was a fixed number of years. More recently, however, the time that a copyright is valid is based on the longevity of the author, plus an additional period of time. These "rules" merit a brief discussion.

Under current law, works published prior to 1 January 1978 are protected for 95 years from the year of first publication. The shorthand expression for this rule is the "95-year" rule. However, there are exceptions whereby a shorter copyright duration might apply, because prior copyright laws required the copyright holder to renew an initial 28-year copyright term. The Copyright Renewal Act of 1992 extended automatic renewal back to works created after 1964 and affirmed the renewal period of 47 years that was set in place by the Copyright Act of 1976 (effective in 1978).

The Copyright Extension Act of 1998 extended the duration of copyright. For works published *since* 1 January 1978 the duration of copyright is the author's lifetime plus 70 years. This sometimes is called the "lifetime plus 70" rule. Joint authorship means that the "lifetime plus 70" rule is applied to the last surviving author.

For corporate and anonymous authors and for work-for-hire publications, copyright protection endures by statute for 95 years from the first date of publication or 120 years from the point of creation, whichever is the shorter period. This may be referred to as the "95/120" rule. These three rules are important to remember in searching for resources in the public domain.

Furthermore, it should be remembered that copyright law varies among nations; not every nation follows U.S. standards and rules. However, the United States is a signatory to international copyright treaties and therefore foreign works are protected similarly to works by U.S. authors.

Permissions and Royalties

During the period of copyright protection anyone who wishes to copy all or part of a work may request permission to do so from the copyright owner. Such requests are made in writing; and publishers grant such requests with written permissions, thus ensuring the accuracy of the exchange.

Requests for "reprint permission," as they are termed, need not be elaborate. They should specify the purpose to which copies of the work will be put, the number of copies to be made, and precisely what is to be copied. Following is a sample template for such a request:

[Date]
Permissions Department
[Publisher's name and address]
Dear Publisher:
I would like permission to reproduce [or reprint] the following for [give reason, such as use in teaching a particular class in school].
Title: [Give complete title, including any subtitle]
Copyright: [Give date and name]
Author: [Give name as it appears on the publication]
Pages to be copied: [Give inclusive page numbers]
Number of copies: [Give number to be printed]
Distribution: [State how copies will be distributed]
Type of copy: [State method of reproduction, such as photocopy]
Please inform me if any fee is required. A stamped, self-addressed envelope is enclosed.
Sincerely,
[Name, title, complete address, and fax number]

The copyright holder has the right to grant permission, with or without charging a fee, or to refuse permission. Many publishers will waive any fee if the permission request is for a short work (or only a few pages from a longer work) and if the copies will be used for legitimate educational purposes. However, it is unreasonable to expect any publisher to grant reprint permission without charging a fee if the reprints will, in essence, duplicate all or a major part of what the publisher is selling. Fees vary widely; but usually they should not exceed a dollar per page, though it can depend on the number of intended copies.

Most publishers respond promptly to reprint requests, some in as little as 24 hours. But it is not unusual for two weeks to pass before a response is forthcoming. Thus it is wise to plan ahead.

Public Domain

I stated at the outset that the public domain comprises two categories of works. The first category is works that have never been copyrighted. This category includes many U.S. government publications, such as public documents and reports generated by various federal departments and agencies.

The second category includes works that once were protected by copyright but whose term of protection has expired. Works published in 1922 or earlier generally fall into this category. Under current law, no new works will enter the public domain until 2019.

A work in the public domain, by definition, is not protected by copyright. It may be reproduced in whole or in part without seeking permission. However, a work in the public domain may not be taken as one's own. Failure to properly credit use of a work in the public domain is a form of plagiarism. Both legally and ethically, anyone who reproduces all or a portion of a work in the public domain is required to credit the work to the original author (if known) and the work's publisher (if applicable).

Works in the public domain seldom are found in bookstores, except perhaps in used-book stores or as reprints. Such works, as a rule, are out of print. Therefore, the places to look for educationally useful works in the public domain are public and university libraries, online library projects, and archives. I will say more about the search for usable works later in this guide.

Derivations and Translations

One significant complication in finding works in the public domain is the effect of derivations and translations. Derivations are new works that are based, in whole or in part, on prior works. Translations are a subcategory of derivations, which also include new editions, revisions, adaptations, and collections consisting of a mix of old and new works.

A caution is needed with regard to translations. A historical work, for example, Plato's essay on education in the *Republic*, can be used freely in its original form without fear of violating copyright. After all, it is more than two thousand years old and, in any case, predates copyright law. On the other hand, a copyrighted 1995 English-language translation of Plato's essay cannot be reprinted without permission, because it is the translation, not the original work, that is protected by the new copyright. The translator (or other copyright owner) would need to be asked for permission to reprint the translation or to use any substantial portion of it.

In principle, no work in the public domain can be given new copyright protection simply by reprinting it. However, a new work based on a work in the public domain is entitled to copyright protection; and it often is difficult to discern where old leaves off and new begins. For example, Robert Louis Stevenson's *Treasure Island* is in the public domain. One can freely reprint it, but the reprint will not take *Treasure Island* out of the public domain. Thus if someone else uses the Stevenson story as the basis for a musical play (or a Muppet movie of recent memory), they are free to do so. The musical play can be copyrighted, however, because it is a derivation.

In some derivations, known as "new versions," it is impossible to separate the new, added material from the old, public domain material. A recent Copyright Office brochure explains the matter as follows:

> In examining a copy (or a record, disk, or tape) for copyright information, it is important to determine whether that particular version of the work is an original edition of the

work or a "new version." New versions include musical arrangements, adaptations, revised or newly edited editions, translations, dramatizations, abridgments, compilations, and works republished with new matter added. The law provides that derivative works, published or unpublished, are independently copyrightable and that the copyright in such a work does not affect or extend the protection, if any, in the underlying work. Under the 1909 law, courts have also held that the notice of copyright on a derivative work ordinarily need not include the dates or other information pertaining to the earlier works incorporated in it. This principle is specifically preserved in the present copyright law. Thus, if the copy (or the record, disk, or tape) constitutes a derivative version of the work, these points should be kept in mind:

- The date in the copyright notice is not necessarily an indication of when copyright in all of the material in the work will expire. Some of the material may already be in the public domain, and some parts of the work may expire sooner than others.
- Even if some of the material in the derivative work is in the public domain and free for use, this does not mean that the "new" material added to it can be used without permission from the owner of copyright in the derivative work. It may be necessary to compare editions to determine what is free to use and what is not.
- Ownership of rights in the material included in a derivative work and in the preexisting work upon which it may be based may differ, and permission obtained from the owners of certain parts of the work may not authorize the use of other parts.

Fair Use

The doctrine of fair use is one of the most debated concepts in copyright law. The question turns on the extent to which a protected work may be copied without the copyright owner's permission.

In principle, no part of a copyrighted work can be reproduced without the copyright owner's specific written permission *except* for single copies of articles to be used for the advancement of scholarly research, short excerpts or quotations to be used in reviews and reports (particularly those by news media), and, under certain circumstances, multiple copies to be used in the classroom.

For fair use, educators must meet the requirement of spontaneity. For example, a teacher might come across an article in the morning newspaper or web page that perfectly illustrates a point of instruction that he or she will be making in that day's lesson. Can the teacher fairly reproduce the article and hand it out to students? Most copyright authorities probably would say yes. The intended use is spontaneous and the teachable moment would be lost were the teacher to seek permission to reproduce the article.

On the other hand, the teacher could not legitimately use the article in another class in the following semester, as the rule of spontaneity would be broken; the teacher would have more than sufficient time to seek reprint permission.

Fair use is a complicated doctrine, and the temptation to violate copyright law arises fairly often in education contexts. For example, teachers sometimes want to incorporate copyrighted material into classroom readers or anthologies. This cannot be done under the fair use doctrine. The preparation of classroom materials cannot be construed as spontaneous. Teachers who want to incorporate copyrighted materials into instructional units need to plan ahead and request the necessary permissions.

This is an important point, and I will elaborate on it in the context of Step 8b as I explain the 8-step procedure for investigating whether a given work is in the public domain.

Investigating Copyright Status: The 8-Step Procedure

My emphasis in this guide is necessarily on the phrase, "in the public domain." Works on a limitless array of subjects can be found in bookstores, libraries, archives, and their online counterparts. However, the real key to locating usable resources for educators is not merely finding the works but ascertaining that they are, indeed, in the public domain and therefore may be reproduced without seeking permission or paying a fee.

Statutory copyright law is contained in Title 17 of the United States Code. Unfortunately, the language of the code is daunting for most readers who are neither copyright experts nor legal scholars. The U.S. Copyright Office provides several publications that offer more reader-friendly information. And, in fact, the Copyright Office provides a method for thoroughly investigating the copyright status of a work; it involves examining a copy of the work and then searching the Catalog of Copyright Entries (CCE) in the Copyright Office. The Copyright Office will make the search for an interested individual for a fee, or one can simply visit the Library of Congress in Washington, D.C., in person to search the catalog. Neither of these alternatives is practical for most educators.

The CCE also can be accessed online through the Library of Congress website (http://lcweb.loc.gov) and the Library of Congress Information System (LOCIS). However, the electronic version of the CCE indexes only works whose copyrights have been registered since 1978, none of which would be in the public domain.

A thorough investigation of copyright status can take eight to 12 weeks, according to the Copyright Office. In order to expedite such an investigation, I have developed an 8-step procedure that focuses on examining works in question without resorting to the CCE. This procedure is designed to explicate the conventions followed by publishers, copyright professionals, and intellectual property professionals so that an effective investigation of copyright can be made with a minimum of effort. Any assumptions are conservative with regard to copyright status in order to avoid the misstep of deciding that a work is in the public domain when, in reality, it is protected by copyright.

The 8-step procedure that I will detail in the following pages includes the following steps:

Step 1. Selecting a Target Work
Step 2. Examining the Work or a Citation
Step 3. Eliminating Government Publications
Step 4. Reviewing Author Biographical Information
Step 5. Eliminating Recently Copyrighted Works
Step 6. Identifying Early Editions in the Public Domain
Step 7. Selecting Alternative Works
Step 8a. Requesting Permission and Paying Fees
Step 8b. Assessing Fair Use

This 8-step procedure obviates the need for experience in investigating copyright status and should be easy for any educator to use. Depending on the nature of the work under investigation, some steps can be skipped. The same is true for certain intended uses of the work. For example, if the reader intends merely to use a short quotation from a work, he or she may be able to skip from Step 1 all the way to Step 8b. But the best way to begin always will be with Step 1. With that in mind, what follows are the details of this 8-step procedure.

Step 1. Selecting a Target Work

A useful work may be spotted in a bookstore, a library, an archive, or online. The reader may have access to a physical or electronic copy of the work, or the work may be noted only as a citation in some index or reference list. In the latter case, one might find a reference to a particular essay that relates to a topic in the curriculum. Rather than go to the trouble of finding an actual copy of the essay only to discover that it is not available in the public domain, the more efficient approach is first to ascertain that the work is in the public domain and then to take the necessary steps to find a copy to reproduce for the class.

The more information one can obtain about a target work, the easier it will be to investigate its copyright status.

Step 2. Examining the Work or a Citation

What does one need to know in order to determine whether the work is protected by copyright or exists in the public domain? To begin, one needs to find out the basics about the work: the name(s) of the author(s), the subject of the work, the title, any subtitle, the publisher, and the place and date of publication. Incidentally, from a copyright standpoint, the editor of a collected work is considered to be the author of the work.

Examining a Physical Copy of the Work. In the case of a book — whether the target work is all or a portion of the book — the easiest way to begin investigating copyright status is physically to examine a copy of the work. In most cases a book's title page or the reverse of the title page will display all of the information that I noted above. Additionally, these pages may include the publisher's address, the edition number (first edition, second edition, etc.), and other information.

The copyright notice usually is given as "Copyright 1960 by Joan James," "© 1960 by Joan James," or "Copyright © 1960 by Joan James." All of these forms are correct. The symbol © is required by the Universal Copyright Convention (UCC) for copyright protection in countries that belong to the UCC but not to the Berne Convention.*

---

*The Berne Convention for the Protection of Literary and Artistic Works, or simply Berne Convention, was incorporated into U.S. copyright law as the Berne Convention Implementation Act of 1988 and required several changes in the Copyright Act of 1976 to eliminate or modify various formalities. Berne Convention formalities do not require the use of the symbol ©.

The term *copyright* also may be seen as an abbreviation: copr. The Buenos Aires Convention, yet another international copyright treaty, requires an additional element that will be found on the reverse title page of many books: "All Rights Reserved."

Corporate works and works made for hire usually carry the name of the publisher or the company, rather than the author, in the copyright notice. An example might be "Copyright © by Milestone Publishing Company."

Another piece of information to be found on the reverse of the title page is the International Standard Book Number, or ISBN. Although this number is not needed specifically for copyright investigation, it can be useful in locating a particular work or its various editions. The counterpart number for periodicals is the International Standard Serial Number, or ISSN.

Examining an Online Copy of the Work. Much of the information that appears on the World Wide Web and its variants is nonstandard. Therefore it may be difficult to find the pertinent information to assist in investigating copyright. Often an online copy of a work is presented as a continuous scroll of pages. Alternatively, it may be structured as a menu, or "tree," so that various sections can be accessed independently, specifically to avoid having to scroll through a longer work. Typical title-page information can be found in at least one of three locations: at the very beginning of the online copy (top of page), at the very end (bottom of page), or on a page in each level of the "tree."

Notice of copyright should appear for works so protected. However, omission of notice does *not* mean that the work is in the public domain; and the inclusion of a solitary date without the full notice should not be construed to represent the copyright date. The date may represent when the author first published the work, when the work was first displayed electronically, or some other time altogether. Online libraries and other repositories often include disclaimers with regard to the copyright status of the works they place online. Thus, absent independent verification, online dates should be regarded with skepticism.

Examining Photographic and Audiovisual Works. Copyright notice for photographic works is similar to that for books and other print publications. The location of the copyright notice may vary, however. Individual photographs may carry the notice within the photographic image, on the margin of the photograph, or on the back of the print. Photographs that are accompanied by print often display the copyright notice somewhere beside the image or at the beginning of the whole work.

Cinemagraphic or videographic works display notice of copyright on their labels and packages, as well as within the work, usually at the beginning or end of the production. Audio works (phonograph records, audiotapes, compact disks, etc.) also display notice of copyright on their labels and packages. The copyright symbol for a sound recording is similar to that for books, except that the C inside the circle is replaced by a P.

Examining a Citation. To begin an investigation of a work's copyright status from a citation, it is important to have the same essential pieces of information that I already have noted above. Standard citations, regardless of "style" (*Chicago Manual of Style, New York Public Library Manual of Style, Publication Manual of the American Psychological Association, MLA Handbook*, and others), contain most, if not all, of the required elements. A typical arrangement of these elements for a book might be: author, title, edition, place of publication, publisher, date of publication. For example:

> Zirkel, Perry A.; Richardson, Sharon Nalbone; and Goldberg, Steven S. *A Digest of Supreme Court Decisions Affecting Education.* Third edition. Bloomington, Ind.: Phi Delta Kappa Educational Foundation, 1995.

For a short story, essay, or article in a collected work, a few more pieces of information are included in the typical citation. For example:

> Blackstone, Tessa. "Good Fortune Counts." In *Against the Tide*, edited by Karen Doyle Walton. Bloomington, Ind.: Phi Delta Kappa Educational Foundation, 1996.

A short story, essay, or article in a periodical would be only slightly different. For example:

Henson, Kenneth T. "Writing for Publication: Some Perennial Mistakes." *Phi Delta Kappan* 78 (June 1997): 781-84.

Articles in a periodical may be protected by copyrighting the entire contents of the periodical, or they may be copyrighted individually by the authors. It will not be possible to tell from a citation who the actual copyright owner is. This is true for all works.

Step 3. Eliminating Government Publications

Most publications of the federal and state governments are not copyrighted because they are produced at public expense and therefore are public documents that are in the public domain. To determine whether a document is a government publication in the public domain, all of the following conditions must be true:

- No individual or corporate author is identified.
- No copyright notice is given.
- The publisher appears to be a government office, agency, or department.

If all of these statements are true, then one can be reasonably assured that the document is in the public domain and usable without permission or the payment of a fee. However, if one or more of the statements is false, then further investigation is warranted.

If an author is credited on the title page or the reverse of the title page, the work may still be a government publication. A work-for-hire authored report, for example, may carry the author's name and still be in the public domain. Or the name on the title page may not be the author at all, but a government official, such as an agency director. Works published by state governments often display the name of the state governor on the title page. None of these names preclude the work being in the public domain.

If the work bears a copyright notice, it may or may not be a government publication; but it certainly is copyrighted. For example, many government publications that reside in the public domain are later republished as derivations with the content of the original government publication supplemented by the addition of commentary or notes that are copyrighted. The contents of the original, uncopyrighted government publication are in the public domain.

The office, agency, or department of government that publishes a work also has a bearing on the work's copyright status. Publications printed by the U.S. Government Printing Office (GPO), for example, generally reside in the public domain because the GPO is tax-supported. By contrast, the United States Postal Service (USPS) is an independent agency of the government that is not tax-supported. Hence the USPS does copyright some of its creative works. Similarly, other agencies, including NASA, copyright their publications but may permit their use for educational purposes.

It is well to remember that the absence of a copyright notice does not mean that a work is not copyrighted. This can happen in the case of documents that appear to be issued by a government agency but, in fact, are publications by nongovernment entities.

A number of for-profit organizations republish government-produced information, sometimes in slightly altered form, and then copyright the new work. Some such organizations have names that make them appear to be government agencies. An example is the Bureau of National Affairs, which, despite its name, is not a government bureau. The way to ensure that the publisher of a work in question is a bona fide government agency is to consult a current directory, such as the National Archive and Records Administration's *United States Government Manual*.

This is the last step if the work in question is an uncopyrighted government publication. If the work appears to be copyrighted but no author is credited, then the next logical move is to proceed to Step 5. Or, if the copyrighted work appears to be a derivation based on a prior government publication, it will make sense to proceed to Step 6 and attempt to locate the original, uncopyrighted work.

Step 4. Reviewing Author Biographical Information

In terms of investigating the copyright status of a work, the primary author-related questions are simple ones: Is the author living or dead? If dead, when did the author die? These questions currently are not pertinent because the "lifetime plus 70" rule of copyright duration does not apply to works published before 1978. Rather, they will serve as guideposts to applying the copyright term limits to works published prior to 1978. The copyright terms on such works lasted from 28 to 95 years from the date of publication.

Generally, works by living authors will not be found in the public domain; therefore, finding that an author is still living may end the investigation. For works by authors now deceased, the second question is telling. Did the author die more than 75 years before 1998? If so, then the work probably — though not certainly — is in the public domain.

The date of an author's death may be given in the preface or introduction to the work, but usually it is found by resorting to a biographical reference of some type. Well-known authors can be found in the most general of reference books, such as an encyclopedia or a dictionary. A more specialized reference is the Contemporary Authors series published by Gale Research. This series is arranged by literary/historical periods. For example, one series deals with works by and about William Shakespeare; another deals with 19th century literature.

The more extensive library catalogs also contain biographical information about authors. For example, the catalogs of the Library of Congress and most major universities incorporate the INNOPAC system from Innovative Interfaces, Inc., which provides up-to-date biographical information. Another example is the catalog of the J. Paul Leonard Library at San Francisco State University, which also is available online at http://www.sfsu.edu. Another excellent online reference is Looksmart International Ltd. at http://www.looksmart.com.

Following are some examples that may be helpful:

20

- Johnson, Jane. (1930-) [or, b. 1930]

This author is living (or was living at the time the reference was published). Even if she is not alive, she certainly did not die more than 75 years before 1998. Therefore her works are copyrighted. To further investigate the possibility of using any of her works in the classroom, the reader should proceed to Step 8a and consider requesting reprint permission.

However, if the reader is not interested in undertaking that time-consuming and perhaps expensive chore, then an alternative would be to move directly to Step 7, Selecting Alternative Works. In either case, Steps 5 and 6 can be skipped.

- James, Edward M. (circa 1820) [or, c. 1820]

The exact dates for this author are unknown. Apparently he lived about (*circa*, or c.) 1820. Certainly he died more than 75 years before 1998. In all likelihood his publications are now in the public domain. Cross-referencing the approximate date in another source would help make this assessment a certainty.

- Jones, John J. (1845-1925) [or b. 1845, d. 1925]

This author is deceased. He died nearly 75 years ago. These facts point to the likelihood that his publications now reside in the public domain. But the evidence is not conclusive because of the duration of copyright laws. For example, if this author copyrighted a work in 1925, the year he died, that copyright would have endured until 1953. An heir holding the copyright could then have renewed the copyright for another 28 years, according to copyright law at that time, thus extending protection until 1981. An automatic extension granted by law in 1978 extended all copyrights an additional 19 years, for a total of 75 years. And a further extension was granted by law in 1998, extending existing copyrights by 20 years. Hence works published more than 75 years before 1998 reside in the public domain

But consider this: What if the copyright heir found an unpublished variation of the 1925 work and published it with a new copyright in 1950? Assume this derivative work is almost indistinguishable from the original. That 1950 copyright would have endured until 1978, 28 years, at which time it would have been automatically renewed for another 47 years, then the standard of the law, thus extending copyright protection until 2025.

In this hypothetical case, the reader would be well-advised to move to Step 6 and look for the original 1925 work, which no longer has copyright protection. However, the original work may no longer be considered the "standard" work by the author if the newer work has gained greater recognition in the meantime. In that case, the reader might want to move to Step 8a and request permission to use the 1950 version that is still protected by copyright.

For a further elaboration of this last point, see Step 6, Identifying Early Editions in the Public Domain.

Step 5. Eliminating Recently Copyrighted Works

This step sounds like common sense, but a couple of wrinkles are worth ironing out.

Works by living authors or authors recently deceased are not in the public domain (unless the author was credited on a government publication, as I explained in Step 3). Step 4 points out that the easiest computation that may lead to finding a work in the public domain is to calculate the publication date plus 75 years — but that is a "rule of thumb," not a legal standard. The duration of copyright has varied from a fixed term based on the year of publication to a term linked to the author's lifetime.

Beginning in 1998, only works published in 1923 and earlier are likely to be in the public domain. This follows the "75-year" rule. However, prior to automatic renewal, the law required the copyright holder to renew the original 28-year copyright. Therefore it is conceivable that copyright protection for a work published in 1936 or earlier *might* have been allowed to expire. By this reasoning, any work bearing a copyright date later than 1936 can be eliminated as *not* in the public domain. Works copyrighted between 1924 and 1936 remain an open question.

Foreign works are yet another matter. Often works published outside the United States are protected for a longer period than the publications of U.S. writers. Standards range from the author's lifetime plus 70 years to a fixed term of 120 years from the date of first publication. The longer term applies to corporate and work-for-hire publications. But any book published after 1900 must be suspected of carrying a valid copyright, and a closer investigation will be warranted.

Again, I point out the pitfalls of translations. While an original work in a foreign language may be in the public domain, a recent English-language translation published in the United States probably will still be protected. For more information about foreign copyrights, it is a good idea to contact the U.S. Copyright Office. Limited space does not permit a detailed discussion in this guide.

Step 6. Identifying Early Editions in the Public Domain

My comment in Step 5 about recent English-language translations applies, of course, to English-language works as well. The reader may need to identify an early edition or early translation that is in the public domain.

When one finds that the target work is copyrighted, it can be helpful to investigate whether an earlier version of the work exists in the public domain that might be as useful as the more recent edition. One clear signal that an earlier edition exists is the presence of an edition number. Sometimes edition numbers are shown on the title page or even incorporated into the title of a book. However, there is no legal requirement to number editions of the same work.

Because the existence of earlier editions of any given work may not be obvious, another way to note the presence of earlier editions is to examine the copyright notice. If the notice, for example, reads "Copyright © 1962, 1998," it is clear that the book has seen two editions (at least). But, again, there is no legal requirement to list the copyright dates of earlier editions.

Incidentally, I should point out that some books also list the number of printings on the reverse of the title page, often near the copyright notice. The number of printings merely refers to how many times the book as been reprinted to fulfill buyers' demands and has no relation to editions of the book.

Even if no edition number appears, it can be helpful to search a library catalog or online database using the author's name to see whether some earlier, no longer copyrighted edition may be available. However, the investigator is cautioned to remember that subsequent editions are published for a couple of reasons. One reason is to continue in print a work of value. In this case only minor revisions may have been made to the original work, perhaps only the addition of a new preface or some explanatory material. Thus the original work may be as useful as any later edition.

Another reason for publishing a new edition of a work is to substantially revise or update the original work. Some information in the earlier edition may be obsolete or just wrong. In this case the original work may be inferior or unusable. For example, John Dewey's *Reconstruction in Philosophy* was published in 1920 by Henry Holt and Company, New York, and undoubtedly entered the public domain at least by 1996, 75 years after the original copyright date. However, an enlarged edition was published by Beacon Press and copyrighted in 1948, during Dewey's lifetime. (He lived from 1859 to 1952). This enlarged edition is still under copyright and undoubtedly is regarded as the "standard" work, given the fact that Dewey himself took a hand in the revision.

When an earlier edition of the work is discovered, the investigator should begin at Step 1 with that publication to ascertain whether it, too, is protected by copyright or has moved into the public domain. If the target work has no earlier edition, the investigator should proceed to Step 7 and select an alternative work.

Step 7. Selecting Alternative Works

When an investigator determines that no earlier edition of a work exists or is available in the public domain, the next step in finding a usable work in the public domain is to select an alternative work.

For many readers a common approach to selecting an alternative work is simply to browse the nearby shelves of a library or bookstore, where works on the same or related subjects might be found. Libraries, in particular, often maintain older works in their collections, and so this method can yield good results. A physical search can be supplemented by browsing the library catalog or collections in used-book stores.

Nowadays technology has provided additional approaches. Keyword searches of library catalogs and online repositories can result in good finds. Well-known titles and long-dead authors can best be found using title and author keywords. For obscure or uncertain titles a subject keyword search may be more productive.

Step 8a. Requesting Permission and Paying Fees

When no alternative work can be found in the public domain, then it may be necessary to investigate using a copyrighted work "by permission," which may mean paying a fee for such use. (An alternative, described as Step 8b, is to determine whether some degree of "fair use" is possible.)

In the previous chapter I provided a sample letter (see page 7) to request permission to use a copyrighted work. Any request for permission should be directed to the copyright owner and should specify the amount (all or selected pages) of the work to be reproduced, how it will be reproduced, the number of copies that will be made, and the purpose of the reproduction. Often, the purpose of the reproduction — commercial, noncommercial, nonprofit, or educational use — will affect whether a fee will be charged or, indeed, whether permission to reprint will be granted at all. Another factor in computing any permission fee will be the amount of the work to be reproduced, for example, a single page or an entire chapter.

Sufficient time for a response to the request for permission must be considered in planning for subsequent use. If the request is sent to a publisher who does not own the copyright, it will need to be forwarded to the actual copyright owner; and that will extend the response time. However, "sufficient time" is no longer necessarily several weeks. In fact, with the advent of fax and e-mail technology, permissions often can be obtained in less than 24 hours.

Permission to use works for educational purposes often can be obtained without a fee, particularly for short excerpts to be reproduced in a limited number of copies. However, permission fees are not unusual for long excerpts, entire chapters, full articles, etc. The typical fee is seldom more than a dollar per page; however, the total fee can become substantial if many pages are sought for reproduction or if a large number of copies will be made. If the copyright holder grants permission, the method of payment (usually to the copyright holder directly or to the Copyright Clearance Center) will be indicated.

Step 8b. Assessing Fair Use

"Fair use" refers to reproducing a portion of a copyrighted work without obtaining permission from the copyright holder or paying a fee. Such use is not recommended without a clear understanding of the legal limitations to fair use. Four factors must be considered in determining fair use:

- The purpose and character of such use, including whether the reproduced material is to be used for a commercial, non-profit, or educational purpose.
- The nature of the copyrighted work.
- The amount of the work to be used in relation to the totality of the work.
- The effect of the use on the potential market for or value of the copyrighted work.

Copyright law permits broader fair use for noncommercial, educational purposes than for profit-making purposes. Thus the Copyright Office has established guidelines for fair use that can be followed by educators at all levels and by librarians and archivists at educational institutions and public libraries. Because fair use standards and copyright law are routinely revisited by the Congress and the courts, users are well-advised to obtain the latest information brochures from the Copyright Office.

Cheryl Besenjak in her book, *Copyright Plain and Simple* (1997), outlines fair use guidelines for classroom teachers, suggesting that for scholarly use or for preparation or delivery of instruction, teachers can legitimately make a *single, personal* copy of:

- A chapter in a book.
- An article from a periodical.
- A short story, essay, or poem.
- A chart, graph, diagram, drawing, or other graphic from a book or periodical.
- A 10-second clip from a video- or audiotape.

A teacher also can make a single, personal copy of a video or audio recording from broadcast television or radio.

Besenjak also suggests that a teacher may make *multiple copies* of these items if the following legal criteria are met:

- The amount of material to be reproduced is brief (substantively limited).
- The copying is done "spontaneously," meaning that the teacher's decision was made on the spur of the moment leaving insufficient time to obtain permission and was not at the direction of others (principal, curriculum director, etc.).
- The cumulative effect is limited — in other words, the teacher is not reproducing a significant number of works as fair use.
- Each copy carries the copyright owner's notice of copyright.
- The number of copies is limited to one class and no more than one per student.

Teachers may not use multiple copying to serve simultaneously taught classes, nor can such copies be used in future classes. Both uses would violate the spontaneity criterion.

"Spontaneity" means just that. For example, if a teacher is preparing a class packet, he or she cannot include materials under the fair use standard. The operative word is *prepare*, which means planning in advance of need. Such planning should include obtaining any necessary permissions. On the other hand, if a teacher spots an article in the morning newspaper that would be perfect to use as part of instruction in his or her first-period class that day, the spontaneity standard of fair use permits the teacher to photocopy and distribute the article to those first-period students.

The "substantive" and "cumulative" limits on multiple copies have been established by the Copyright Office as follows:

Substantive Limits

Maximum Quantity	Description
1 illustration	Multiple copying of an illustration from a book or serial issue.
250 words or 2 pages	Multiple copying of a complete poem.
250 words	Multiple copying of an excerpt from a poem or poetry.
2,500 words	Multiple copying of a complete article, short story, or essay.
1,000 words or 10% of words	Multiple copying of an excerpt from a prose work.
10% of words or 2 pages	Multiple copying of a work that combines language with illustrations.

Cumulative Limits

Maximum Quantity	Description
0 instance	Multiple copying of videographic or phonographic work.
1 instance	Multiple copying of complete brief work (that is, less than 250 words) per author.
2 instances	Multiple copying of excerpts per author.
3 instances	Multiple copying of excerpts per collection (or anthology) or periodical volume.
9 instances	Multiple copying of any copyrighted work per class per semester.

Summary and Examples

This 8-step procedure is relatively quick and comprehensive. It follows a logical sequence that should guide the investigator to rapidly separate the usable works from the unusable and to identify those public domain (or affordably available) resources that can be reproduced for use in research and instruction. Even though applying the 8 steps is a fairly straightforward procedure, a few examples may be helpful.

Government Document Example. Publications of the United States government include periodicals, various types of reports, and books. Most are printed by the Government Printing Office (GPO), but they may be distributed by either the GPO or the agency that produced them. Government documents also are distributed through other organizations, such as the National Technical Information Service (NTIS). Although a government document may be in the public domain, both the GPO and NTIS usually charge a fee to cover the cost of printing and distribution. Government documents on the Internet often are free. Following are two examples related to investigating actual government publications and publications that resemble government publications. The first example is an actual government document.

Step 1. Selecting a Target Work.
Census of Population and Housing, 1990.

Step 2. Examining the Work or a Citation.
The work was issued by the Bureau of the Census, Department of Commerce, in 1994.

Step 3. Eliminating Government Publications.
An inspection of the work, particularly the front and back of the title page, reveals no author and no copyright notice. The publisher is a department of the federal government. Therefore the work is a government publication and resides in the public domain. Remaining steps may be omitted.

The next example is a document that resembles a government publication.

Step 1. Selecting a Target Work.
Planning for the 1990 Census: Priorities for Research and Testing. Interim Report, 1984.

Step 2. Examining the Work or a Citation.
The "author" of the work is listed as the National Research Council. The work was published by National Academy Press, Inc., in 1984.

Step 3. Eliminating Government Publications.
An inspection of the title page reveals a copyright notice, and the publisher is a corporation, not a government agency. This last point is confirmed by quickly looking up the publisher in the agency list of the United States Government Manual, where, of course, it cannot be found. Therefore this publication cannot be eliminated from further investigation.

Step 4. Reviewing Author Biographical Information.
This step is not applicable because the author is an organization, not an individual.

Step 5. Eliminating Recently Copyrighted Works.
Because this work carries a 1984 copyright, it will not come into the public domain for many years.

Step 6. Identifying Early Editions in the Public Domain.
The work in question is a first edition. Also, the timely nature of the work precludes the likelihood of using an earlier edition.

Step 7. Selecting Alternative Works.
The recency of the work suggests that few, if any, alternatives may exist; however, a search of government publications on the same subject might be productive.

Step 8a. Requesting Permission and Paying Fees.
If a substantial portion is desired for reproduction, a request for permission to reprint should be directed to National Academy Press.

Step 8b. Assessing Fair Use.
If only a small part of the work is desired, it might fall legitimately under the fair use guidelines.

Anthology Example. Anthologies are collections of works, fiction or nonfiction, usually by various authors. The individual works may have been published elsewhere prior to being collected in the anthology. Therefore some or all of the collected works may reside in the public domain, even though the anthology itself carries a recent copyright date. The anthology date pertains only to new material, such as an introduction, and not to the existing works. Following is an example that may be helpful.

Step 1.　Selecting a Target Work.
The Great Educators: Readings for Leaders in Education, 1972.

Step 2.　Examining the Work or a Citation.
The editors of this work are Hugh C. Black, Kenneth V. Lottich, and Donald S. Seckinger. It was published by Nelson-Hall Company in 1972.

Step 3.　Eliminating Government Publications.
This work lists the authors. It has a copyright notice. And it is published by a private company. Hence it is not a government publication.

Step 4.　Reviewing Author Biographical Information.
The biographical information for the editors is immaterial, because the recency of publication means that the work will be protected by copyright for many years yet. However, a number of the essays included in the anthology are by historical figures who are sufficiently old that the essays are likely to have expired copyrights. One of these essays is an excerpt from a longer work by Horace Mann, who lived from 1796 to 1859.

Step 5.　Eliminating Recently Copyrighted Works.
The Mann excerpt is from *The Massachusetts System of Common Schools*, published in 1846. Clearly it is in the public domain and can be reproduced without further investigation. But another essay in the anthology is an excerpt (actually Chapter 6) from *How We Think* by John Dewey, who lived from 1859 to 1952. This work was copyrighted first in 1910; a second edition was copyrighted in 1933 and used in the anthology "by

permission of the publishers." The 1933 version of the book, published during Dewey's lifetime, likely is still protected by copyright.

Step 6. Identifying Early Editions in the Public Domain.
In all likelihood the 1910 edition of Dewey's work resides in the public domain; it passes the test for copyright duration because it was published 75 years prior to 1998. However, if it differs substantially from the 1933 edition, it may not be considered standard or authoritative, particularly because the 1933 edition was produced by the original author.

Step 7. Selecting Alternative Works.
Unless it is essential to use a work by John Dewey, one might turn to other writers on education to complement the essay by Horace Mann. The anthology in question, for example, also includes works by Herbert Spencer (1820-1903), William T. Harris (1835-1909), and Francis W. Parker (1837-1902), all of which are in the public domain.

Step 8a. Requesting Permission and Paying Fees.
If one wants to reproduce a substantial excerpt from the 1933 edition of the Dewey work, then a request for reprint permission can be sent to D.C. Heath and Company in Boston, which is listed as the publisher.

Step 8b. Assessing Fair Use.
If one wants to use only a brief quotation from the Dewey work, then it might be fair use. As in other examples, the standards of spontaneity, substantiality, and cumulativity will apply.

Book Example. Works of fiction — novels, plays, poems — and nonfiction — textbooks, reference books — can be treated in the same fashion as individual works within an anthology. For example:

Step 1. Selecting a Target Work.
         Emma, 1950.

Step 2. Examining the Work or a Citation.
         This book by Jane Austen was spotted in a 1950 edition published by J.M. Dent and Sons.

Step 3. Eliminating Government Publications.
         This book is not a government publication.

Step 4. Reviewing Author Biographical Information.
         Jane Austen lived from 1775 to 1817, and *Emma* was published in 1816.

Step 5. Eliminating Recently Copyrighted Works.
         Recency of publication means that the 1950 edition of *Emma* still is protected by copyright. It cannot be used without permission, though the copyright applies only to new material added since the previous edition.

Step 6. Identifying Early Editions in the Public Domain.
         Virtually any edition of *Emma* published prior to 1923 (75 years prior to 1998) will be in the public domain. For example, an Everyman's Series edition was published in 1906, and several earlier editions can be found in libraries and archives, any of which could be reproduced without obtaining permission. Given these options, the investigation can end with this step.

The following flow chart offers a visual summary of the 8-step procedure.

The 8-Step Procedure

```
                    ┌────────────────────────────┐
                    │             1              │
                    │   Selecting a Target Work   │
                    └────────────────────────────┘
                                 │
                                 ▼
        ┌──────────────────────────────────────┐   No      ┌──────────┐
        │                  2                   │ Copyright  │  Public  │
    ───▶│    Examining the Work or a Citation   │ ────────▶ │  Domain  │
        └──────────────────────────────────────┘           └──────────┘
                                 │
                                 ▼
                 ┌──────────────────────────────────────┐
                 │                   3                   │
                 │   Eliminating Government Publications  │
                 └──────────────────────────────────────┘
                                 │
                                 ▼
  Living Author  ┌──────────────────────────────────────────┐
                 │                     4                     │
                 │   Reviewing Author Biographical Information │
                 └──────────────────────────────────────────┘
                                 │
                                 ▼
  "75 year" rule ┌──────────────────────────────────────────┐
                 │                     5                     │
                 │    Eliminating Recently Copyrighted Works   │
                 └──────────────────────────────────────────┘
                                 │
                                 ▼
        ┌──────────────────────────────────────┐  Expired   ┌──────────┐
        │                  6                   │ Copyright  │  Public  │
        │   Identifying Early Editions of the Work │ ───────▶ │  Domain  │
        └──────────────────────────────────────┘           └──────────┘
                                 │
                                 ▼
        ┌──────────────────────────────────────┐
    ───▶│                  7                   │
        │       Selecting Alternative Works      │
        └──────────────────────────────────────┘
                                 │
              ┌──────────────────┴──────────────────┐
              ▼                                      ▼
┌──────────────────────────────┐      ┌──────────────────────────────┐
│              8a              │      │              8b              │
│ Requesting Permission and Paying Fees │  │       Assessing Fair Use        │
└──────────────────────────────┘      └──────────────────────────────┘
```

Locating Works
in the
Public Domain

Previously I sketched some strategies for locating works that may be in the public domain. This section provides a brief amplification of those strategies.

Public and University Libraries

Large, well-established public and university libraries represent a good place to locate public domain works, especially for readers who may not have computer access to online repositories and archives. Even when such access is available, the library collections represent an excellent source of useful material for educational purposes.

Libraries have many public domain works in their collections because they often maintain early editions of works even when newer editions are available, and they often retain older books in circulation long after they are out of print and cannot be found in bookstores. Archives often specialize in older works and so can be a gold mine for instructional resources; however, many archives do not maintain (or keep very few) circulating copies. Instead, they often supplement access by providing copy services for materials that do not circulate.

In most libraries today, electronic cataloging has replaced the card catalog drawers of past decades. The electronic catalogs are easy to use and may even contain more information than the old card catalogs did. However, there can be drawbacks to the electronic catalog if a library has not converted all of its data to that form. Some libraries catalog only holdings acquired since a certain date, such as 1970. Thus older books may not show up in the electronic catalog though they are in the collection; they can be found only by searching the card catalog drawers or, in some cases, only by browsing the stacks. Eventually, most of these older works will be entered into the electronic catalog; but a collection of many thousands of books takes a long time to catalog, and some libraries are still working through that effort.

The best resource in any library often is its staff of reference librarians, who can help the interested reader to find sought-after materials. In many cases a phone call in advance of a visit can be highly productive.

Online Repositories

The Internet has become a formidable resource for educators. The term "online repositories" covers a variety of electronic libraries and archives. Many specialize in public domain works, some of which can be accessed in whole-text versions. Others provide complete citations and source information, often including abstracts that will help the reader decide which originals are worth investigating.

University-based and government-sponsored online repositories are largely nonprofit entities, though some are spinoffs of university projects. Also, some may be maintained by individuals engaged in a project, such as university students.

Accessing online repositories is different from searching library catalogs because few online repositories use traditional cataloging protocols, such as the Dewey Decimal System or the Library of Congress (LC) classification systems. Some online repositories organize their collections by subject areas, but these generally are less extensive than in traditional cataloging systems. More typically, the online resources require keyword searches of their collections, using author, title, or subject keywords. For example, the Internet Public Library of the School of Information at the

University of Michigan and Project Gutenburg both have impressive online catalogs of large databases. The databases feature a sophisticated search capability that can automatically generate a list of works that reside in the public domain for any given author or title keyword. A list of some of the many online repositories can be found in the Resources section that follows.

Other — albeit less productive — online resources are the electronic bookstores, such as the online version of Barnes and Noble (http://www.barnesandnoble.com) and the exclusively online bookstore Amazon.com (http://www.amazon.com). Like physical bookstores, however, the online bookstores sell books whose recency of copyright precludes free use. However, they also sell reprints that may lead to earlier versions in the public domain.

Photocopy Services for Out-of-Print Publications

Some works that reside in the public domain are not available locally or conveniently through interlibrary loan. But these works may be available at a cost from one of the specialized organizations that provides copies of out-of-print publications. For example, the Document Center at the Library of the University of Michigan is a well-known organization that reproduces out-of-print works. After receiving permission from the publisher of a work, the Document Center photocopies the work and distributes the payment of the royalty fee to the publisher or to the Copyright Clearance Center (CCC). The Document Center is listed in the Resources section.

Final
Thoughts

This guide provides basic information about copyright and straightforward strategies for investigating whether a work is protected by copyright or available in the public domain. The 8-step procedure will be useful for novices and experienced investigators alike.

The 8-step procedure is designed to help educators and others avoid inadvertently infringing on copyright, which can result in costly legal liability. It also will help instructors who desire to make up course packets, because they can determine well in advance which materials will require written permission to reproduce and which are in the public domain. Commercial printers, on whom instructors often call to print course packets, have become very cautious because of lawsuits; and most now insist that instructors present written permissions before they will print a packet.

I would caution educators not to rely on the doctrine of fair use. Fair use is specifically limited, and it is wiser to plan ahead. In fact, good planning can lead to using primarily or exclusively works in the public domain. Where copyrighted works must be used, good planning also provides time to secure the necessary permissions.

The process of finding works, especially derivations, in the public domain could be greatly simplified if all published works included a comprehensive copyright notice on the reverse of the title page. For example, this notice might state precisely the material within the work for which the author claims copyright and which is derived from an earlier work. Then a reader could be confident about obtaining just that material that resides in the public domain. Unfortunately, the copyright information typically included with most published works is not this expansive. Thus the 8-step procedure in this brief guide provides a helpful tool for finding those works that are most accessible for instructional purposes. My hope is that it offers a key to the treasures of the public domain.

Resources

This guide includes a list of valuable resources, all of which can be accessed online. The conventional contact information, including telephone number, also is provided for those without access to the Internet. The resource types include copyright information resources, general reference works, public and university library resources, online collections and repositories, and guide lists of educational sites.

The resources that follow are not a complete list of what is available to educators. However, they do provide a good starting place for the search for materials in the public domain. It is important to remember that most of these resources contain both copyrighted works and public domain holdings. Very few resources, including government agencies, contain only resources that are in the public domain.

Copyright Information

Association of American Publishers. *The Copyright Primer*. Washington, D.C. (202) 232-3335. http://www.publishers.org

Besenjak, Cheryl. *Copyright Plain and Simple*. N.J.: Career Press, 1997.

Copyright Office. *Circular No. 1*. Washington, D.C.: Library of Congress, 1991 *et seq*. (202) 707-6850. http://lcweb.loc.gov/copyright

Copyright Law Library. *Nimmer on Copyright*. Release 44. New York: Matthew Bender & Co., 1997.

Fishman, Stephen. *The Copyright Handbook: How to Protect and Use Written Works*. 4th ed. Berkeley, Calif.: Nolo Press, 1998. http://www.nolo.com

Institute for Learning Technologies. *ILT Guide to Copyright*. New York: Columbia University Institute for Learning Technologies, 1998. http://deamon.ilt.columbia.edu/projects/copyright/index.html

Kerber, R. "Vigilant Copyright Holders Patrol the Internet." *Wall Street Journal*, 5 December 1995, p. B1.

Legal Information Institute. *Copyright Law Materials*. Ithaca, N.Y.: Cornell University Legal Information Institute, 1998. http://www.law.cornell.edu/topics/copyright.html

Nimmer, M.B. *Treatise on Copyright*. New York: Matthew Bender & Co., 1997.

Strong, William. *The Copyright Book*. 4th ed. Cambridge, Mass.: MIT Press, 1992. http://mitpress.mit.edu

"Title 17." *United States Code Service [USCS]*. N.J.: Lawyer's Cooperative, 1998.

U.S. Copyrights. File 120. Dialog Corporation, 1998. http://library.dialog.com

Reference Works

Books-in-Print. New York: R.R. Bowker. http://www.bowker.com

Contemporary Authors Series, 1950-Present. Detroit: Gale Research. (313) 961-2242. http://www.gale.com

Hoppe, A.J. *The Reader's Guide to Everyman's Library*. No. 887. London: J.M. Dent; New York: E.P. Dutton, 1962.

Jody, Marilyn, and Saccardi, Marianne. *Computer Conversations: Readers and Books Online*. Urbana. Ill.: National Council of Teachers of English, 1996.

Leshin, Cynthia. *Internet Adventures: A Step-by-Step Guide for Finding and Using Educational Resources*. New York: Allyn & Bacon, 1996. 1-800-278-3525.

Polly, Jean. *Internet Kids and Family Yellow Pages*. 2nd ed. Palo Alto, Calif.: Osborne/McGraw-Hill, 1997. http://www.netmom.com

United States Government Manual 1998-99. Washington, D.C.: Office of the Federal Register, National Archives and Records Administration. http://www.access.gpo/nara

National Libraries, Archives, Information Services, and Associations

American Bar Association
Intellectual Property Law Section (IPL)
750 N. Lake Shore Drive
Chicago, IL 60611
(312) 988-5000
http://www.abanet.org

American Library Association (ALA)
50 East Huron
Chicago, IL 60611
1-800-545-2433 or (312) 440-9374
http://www.ala.org

Copyright Clearance Center (CCC)
CCC Online
Academic Licensing Services
222 Rosewood Drive
Danvers, MA 01923
http://www.copyright.com

Digital Library Federation (DLF)
http://lcweb.loc.gov/loc/ndlf

The Document Center
University of Michigan Library
Ann Arbor, MI 48109
(734) 764-0410
http://www.lib.umich.ed/libhome/Documents.center/index.html

Library of Congress (LC)
101 Independence Ave., S.E.
Washington, DC 20540
http://www.loc.gov

National Educational Computing Association (NECA)
http://cate.uoregon.edu/necc

National Archives and Records Administration (NARA)
8601 Adelphi Road
College Park, MD 20740
(718) 647-8109
http://www.nara.gov

National Technical Information Service (NTIS)
U.S. Department of Commerce
Springfield, VA 22161
(703) 605-6050 or (703) 321-8547
http://www.ntis.gov/search.htm

United States Government Printing Office (GPO)
Superintendent of Documents
P.O. Box 371954
Pittsburgh, PA 15250-7954
(202) 512-1800 or 1-888-293-6498
http://www.gpo.gov

Online Digital Libraries, Electronic Text Archives, and Repositories

The reader should note that resources marked with an asterisk contain a significant quantity of works that reside in the public domain. Other listed resources contain some works that reside in the public domain.

Internet Public Library (IPL)*
School of Information
University of Michigan
304 West Hall
550 East University Avenue
Ann Arbor, MI 48109-1092
(734) 763-2285 or (734) 764-2475
http://www.ipl.org

Project Gutenberg*
P.O. Box 2782
Champaign, IL 61825
http://www.promo.net/pg

On-line Books Page*
Carnegie Mellon University
http://www.cs.cmu.edu/books.html

The Universal Library Project *
Carnegie Mellon University
http://www.ul.cs.cmu.edu

Project Bartleby Archive*
Columbia University
http://www.cc.columbia.edu/acis/bartleby

Cornell Digital Library Project
Cornell University
http://moa.cit.cornell.edu

Duke Papyrus Archive
Duke University
http://scriptorium.lib.duke.edu/papyrus

Emory Virtual Library Project
Emory University
http://www.library.emory.edu/VL/vlhome.html

Center for Electronic Projects in American Culture Studies
    (CEPACS)
Georgetown University
http://www.georgetown.edu/tamlit/info/cepacs.html

Harvard Information Infrastructure Project
John F. Kennedy School of Government
79 John F. Kennedy Street
Cambridge, MA 02138
(617) 496-1389
http://ksgwww.harvard.edu/iip

American Memory: Historical Collections for the National
    Digital Library
Library of Congress
http://lcweb2.loc.gov/ammem

Complete Works of William Shakespeare*
Massachusetts Institute of Technology
http://the-tech.mit.edu/Shakespeare/works.html

The Internet Classics Archive
MIT Program in Writing and Humanistic Studies
Massachusetts Institute of Technology
http://classics.mit.edu

NYPL Online
New York Public Library
Fifth Avenue and 42nd Street
New York, NY 10018-2788
(212) 930-0740
http://www.nypl.org/online.html

Oxford Text Archive (OTA)
Oxford University
13 Banbury Road, Oxford, OX2 6NN
Oxfordshire, United Kingdom
http://firth.natcorp.ox.ac.uk/ota/public/index.shtml

Princeton Library of Electronic Texts in the Humanities (PLETH)
Princeton University Library
http://infoshare1.princeton.edu:2003/digital collections

Center for Electronic Texts in the Humanities (CETH)
Rutgers University
169 College Avenue
New Brunswick, NJ 08903
http://www.ceth.rutgers.edu

Stanford University Digital Libraries Project
Stanford University
http://www.diglib.stanford.edu/diglib/pub

UC Berkeley Digital Library Sunsite
UC Berkeley
http://sunsite.berkeley.edu/R+D/ucblibrary.html

ARTFL Project*
University of Chicago
http://humanities.uchicago.edu/ARTFL/ARTFL.html

Digital Library Initiatives (DLI)
University of Michigan, Ann Arbor
http://www.lib.umich.edu/libhome/DLI

Humanities Text Initiative
School of Information
University Library and University of Michigan Press
http://www.hti.umich.edu

Center for Electronic Text and Images (CETI)
University of Pennsylvania
http://www.library.upenn.edu/etext

Perseus Project
Tufts University
http://www.perseus.tufts.edu

Project Open Book
Yale University Library
http://www.library.yale.edu/preservation/pobweb.htm

Electronic Text Center*
Alderman Library
University of Virginia.
(804) 924-3230
Fax: (804) 924-1431
http://etext.lib.virginia.edu

An Online Library of Literature*
http://www.literature.org

The New Bartleby Library
http://www.bartleby.com

Resource Guides

Federal Resources for Education Excellence (FREE)
Washington, D.C.: U.S. Department of Education
1-800-872-5327
http://www.ed.gov/free

Looksmart Internet Directory
Looksmart International Ltd. New York: 1998.
http://www.looksmart.com

Internet Adventures Newsletter
XPLORA Publishing Company
Phoenix, AZ
1-800-800-2775
www.xplora.com/xplora

Literature Online (LION)
Chadwyck-Healey, Ltd.
London.
http://lion.chadwyck.com

Classroom Connect
1-800-638-1639
www.classroom.com

Computing Learning Newsletter
Computer Learning Foundation, Inc.
Palo Alto, CA
(650) 327-3347
www.computerlearning.org

About the Author

Kenyon D. Potter is a professional engineer, educator, and writer in California. He received his bachelor of science degree from the Massachusetts Institute of Technology and a master of science from the University of California at Berkeley. Potter currently is attending law school in California while continuing to practice as a civil engineer.

Potter has written and made presentations on earthquake behavior. He also has designed exhibits and devices to demonstrate aspects of earthquake behavior to educators and the public.